PLEASE TAKE MY KIDS!

The Greatest Quotes

for Parents with Children from Hell

by: Torran Bagamary and Michelle Iglesias

CCC Books

PO Box 1827

Westfield, MA 01086

by: Torran Bagamary and Michelle Iglesias
Copyright © 2008 CCC Books
All rights reserved

Published in the U.S.A. by CCC Books
PO Box 1827, Westfield, MA 01086
(413) 214-4770
stores.lulu.com/cccbooks

ISBN # 978-0-6152-0653-0

In memory of Michael B. Lynn

And his three loving dogs,

Chewy, Chuck and Cheese

Any astronomer can predict

with absolute accuracy

just where every star in the universe

will be at 11:30 tonight.

He can make no such prediction

about his teenage daughter.

James T. Adams

Smack your children every day.

If you don't know why—he does.

Joey Adams

It's a sad moment, really,

when parents first become a bit

frightened of their children.

Ama Ata Aidoo

It is no wonder that people

are so horrible

when they start life as children.

Kingsley Amis

A characteristic of the normal child is he doesn't act that way very often.

Anonymous

A child's greatest period of growth is the month after you've purchased new school clothes.

Anonymous

A father is someone who carries pictures where his money used to be.

Anonymous

A little girl is sugar and spice and everything nice – especially when she's taking a nap.

Anonymous

A lot of growing up takes place between

"It fell" and "I dropped it."

Anonymous

A teenager is always too tired

to hold a dishcloth, but

never too tired to hold a phone.

Anonymous

Adolescence is a period of rapid changes.

Between the ages of 12 and 17,

for example,

a parent ages as much as 20 years.

Anonymous

Anyone who says

"Easy as taking candy from a baby"

has never tried it.

Anonymous

By the time a girl becomes a teenager,

her parents are so old

that she cannot do anything with them.

Anonymous

Child, n.: a noise with dirt on it.

Anonymous

Child rearing myth #1:

Labor ends when the baby is born.

Anonymous

Children are natural mimics

who act like their parents,

despite every effort to

teach them good manners.

Anonymous

Children seldom misquote you.

In fact, they usually repeat word for word

what you shouldn't have said.

Anonymous

Everyone is in awe of the lion tamer

in a cage with half a dozen lions—

everyone but a school bus driver.

Anonymous

Give me a child for the first seven years, and you may do what you like with him afterwards.

Anonymous

Grandchildren are God's reward for not killing your kids.

Anonymous

I love to give homemade gifts.

Which one of my kids do you want?

Anonymous

It's funny that those things your kids did that got on your nerves seem so cute when your grandchildren do them.

Anonymous

Kids use to ask where they came from, now they tell you where to go.

Anonymous

Learn from your parents' mistakes— use birth control.

Anonymous

Little girl's definition of conscience: Something that makes you tell your mother before your brother or sister does.

Anonymous

Mothers of teens know why some animals eat their young.

Anonymous

My kids are the reason for everything.

The reason everything

is out of place, broken, and dirty.

Anonymous

Neither teenagers nor cats

turn their heads

when you call them by name.

Anonymous

Raising a child is like baking a cake—

by the time you find out it's a disaster;

it's too late.

Anonymous

The main purpose

of holding children's parties

is to remind yourself

that there are children

more awful than your own.

Anonymous

There is nothing wrong with teenagers that trying to reason with them won't aggravate.

Anonymous

Today's children would be less spoiled if we could spank grandparents.

Anonymous

Too many parents are not on spanking terms with their children.

Anonymous

We childproofed our home 3 years ago and they're still getting in.

Anonymous

We never know the true joy of happiness until we have kids—then it's too late.

Anonymous

What you don't know takes a lot of explaining to children.

Anonymous

Youth is when you blame

all your troubles on your parents;

Maturity is when you learn

that everything is the fault

of the younger generation.

Anonymous

It is the duty of the children

to wait on elders,

and not the elders on children.

African Proverb

Raising children is like

chewing on a stone.

Arab Proverb

The American Dream

is not to own your home

but to get your kids out of it.

Dick Armey

Raising kids is

part joy and part guerilla warfare.

Ed Asner

Don't try to make children

grow up to be like you,

or they do it.

Russell Baker

I believe that we parents must encourage our children to become educated, so they can get into a good college that we cannot afford.

Dave Barry

I've noticed that one thing about parents is that no matter what stage your child is in, the parents who have older children always tell you the next stage is worse.

Dave Barry

To an adolescent,

there is nothing in the world

more embarrassing than a parent.

Dave Barry

Children have never been very good

at listening to their elders,

but they have never failed

to imitate them.

James Baldwin

You see much more of your children once they leave home.

Lucille Ball

Experts say you should never hit your children in anger. When is a good time? When you're feeling festive?

Roseanne Barr

When my husband comes home,

if the kids are still alive,

I figure I've done my job.

Roseanne Barr

Children are unpredictable.

You never know what inconsistency

they are gong to catch you in next.

Henry Ward Beecher

In America

there are two classes of travel—

first class, and with children.

Robert Benchley

The most effective form

of birth control I know

is spending the day with my kids.

Jill Bensley

It is amazing how quickly the kids learn to drive a car, yet are unable to understand the lawnmower, snow-blower, or vacuum cleaner.

Ben Berger

If evolution really works, how come mothers only have two hands?

Milton Berle

If you want to recapture your youth,

just cut off his allowance.

Al Bernstein

There are two things in life

for which we are never truly prepared:

Twins.

Josh Billings

Have you any idea how many kids it takes to turn off one light in the kitchen? Three. It takes one to say, "What light?" and two more to say, "I didn't turn it on."

Erma Bombeck

I have a very practical view of raising children. I put a sign in each of their rooms: "Checkout Time is in 18 years."

Erma Bombeck

In general my children refuse to eat anything that hasn't danced in television.

Erma Bombeck

It goes without saying that you should never have more children than you have car windows.

Erma Bombeck

My kids always perceived the bathroom as a place where you wait it out until all the groceries are unloaded from the car.

Erma Bombeck

Never lend your car to anyone to whom you have given birth.

Erma Bombeck

One thing they never told you about child raising is that for the rest of your life, at the drop of a hat, you are expected to know your child's name and how old he or she is.

Erma Bombeck

When my kids become wild and unruly, I use a nice safe playpen. When they're finished, I climb out.

Erma Bombeck

Youngsters of the age of two or three are endowed with extraordinary strength. They can lift a dog twice their own weight and dump him into a bathtub.

Erma Bombeck

There was a time when we expected nothing of our children but obedience, as opposed to the present, when we expect everything of them but obedience.

Anatole Broyard

Children are contemptuous, haughty, irritable, envious, sneaky, selfish, lazy, flighty, timid, liars and hypocrites, quick to laugh and cry, extreme in expressing joy and sorrow, especially about trifles, they'll do anything to avoid pain but they enjoy inflicting it: little men already.

Jean de La Bruyère

People who say they sleep like a baby usually don't have one.

Leo J. Burke

Happiness is having

a large, loving, close-knit family

in another city.

George Burns

Children really brighten up a household—

they never turn the lights off.

Ralph Bus

Parents are the last people on earth who ought to have children.

Samuel Butler

Never raise your hands to your kids.

It leaves your groin unprotected.

Red Buttons

Learning to dislike children at an early age saves a lot of expense and aggravation later in life.

Robert Byrne

Young people should be helped, sheltered, ignored, and clubbed if necessary.

Al Capp

The other night

I ate at a real nice family restaurant.

Every table had an argument going.

George Carlin

You see,

money isn't everything in life is it?

But it keeps you in touch

with your children.

Johnnie Casson

Parents who are afraid to put their foot down usually have children who step on their toes.

Chinese Proverb

Rashness belongs to youth; prudence to old age.

Marcus Tullius Cicero

Why do grandparents and grandchildren get along so well? They have the same enemy—the mother.

Claudette Colbert

It is not a bad thing that children should occasionally, and politely, put parents in their place.

Sidonie G. Colette

Parents:

persons who spend half their time worrying how a child will turn out, and the rest of the time wondering when a child will turn in.

Ted Cook

Always end the name of your child with a vowel, so that when you yell the name will carry.

Bill Cosby

Having a child is surely

the most beautiful irrational act

that two people in love can commit.

Bill Cosby

Human beings are the only creatures

that allow their children

to come back home.

Bill Cosby

I guess the real reason

that my wife and I had children

is the same reason

that Napoleon had for invading Russia:

it seemed like a good idea at the time.

Bill Cosby

Whenever your kids are out of control,

you can take comfort from the thought

that even God's omnipotence

did not extend to His kids.

Bill Cosby

Children in a family are like flowers in a bouquet: there's always one determined to face the opposite direction from the way the arranger desires.

Marcelene Cox

Parenthood: The state of being better chaperoned than you were before marriage.

Marcelene Cox

There are three ways to get something done: do it yourself, employ someone, or forbid your children to do it.

Monta Crane

The trouble with children is they're not returnable.

Quentin Crisp

The first half of our life

is ruined by our parents

and the second half by our children.

Clarence Darrow

A happy childhood

has spoiled many a promising life.

Robertson Davies

If you have never been hated

by your child,

you have never been a parent.

Bette Davis

In the little world

in which children have their existence,

who's ever bring them up,

there is nothing so finely perceived

and so finely felt as injustice.

Charles Dickens

All children are essentially criminal.

Dennis Diderot

I think we're seeing in working a change from "Thank God it's Friday" to "Thank God it's Monday." If any working mother has not experienced that feeling, her children are not adolescent.

Ann Diehl

There are times when parenthood seems nothing more than feeding the hand that bites you.

Ann Diehl

Always be nice to your children because they are the ones who will choose your rest home.

Phyllis Diller

Cleaning your house

while your kids are still growing up

is like shoveling the walk

before it stops snowing.

Phyllis Diller

Most children threaten at times

to run away from home.

This is the only thing

that keeps some parents going.

Phyllis Diller

Tranquilizers work only if you follow the advice on the bottle— keep away from children.

Phyllis Diller

We spend the first twelve months of our children's lives teaching them to walk and talk and the next twelve teaching them to sit down and shut up.

Phyllis Diller

I believe in smacking children—

I just use a cattle prod.

Jenny Eclair

Premature burial works just fine

as a cure for adolescence.

George Alec Effinger

You have a wonderful child.

Then, when he's 13,

gremlins carry him away

and leave in his place a stranger

who gives you not a moment's peace.

Jill Eikenberry

A child is a curly dimpled lunatic.

Ralph Waldo Emerson

There was never a child so lovely

but his mother was glad

to get him to sleep.

Ralph Waldo Emerson

Children suck the mother

when they are young

and the father

when they are old.

English Proverb

A successful parent is one who raises a child who grows up and is able to pay for his or her own psychoanalysis.

Nora Ephron

Any child can tell you that the sole purpose of a middle name is so he can tell when he's really in trouble.

Dennis Fakes

The hand that rocks the cradle usually is attached to someone who isn't getting enough sleep.

John Fiebig

When children are doing nothing, they are doing mischief.

Henry Fielding

Madam, there's no such thing as a tough child— if you parboil them for seven hours, they always come out tender.

W.C. Fields

Insomnia: A contagious disease often transmitted from babies to parents.

Shannon Fife

The persons hardest to convince that they're at the retirement age are children at bedtime.

Shannon Fife

Teach your child to hold his tongue.

He'll learn fast enough to speak.

Benjamin Franklin

I have just returned

from a children's party.

I'm one of the survivors.

Percy French

Children are completely egotistic;

they feel their needs intensely

and strive ruthlessly to satisfy them.

Sigmund Freud

Having one child makes you a parent;

having two, you are a referee.

David Frost

It is dangerous

to confuse children with angels.

David Fyfe

Anyone who thinks the art of conversation is dead ought to tell a child to go to bed.

Robert Gallagher

If children grew up according to early indication, we should have nothing but geniuses.

Johann Wolfgang Von Goethe

It is not giving children more

that spoils them;

it is giving the more

to avoid confrontation.

John Gray

Alas! Regardless of their doom,

The little victims play;

No sense have they of ills to come,

Nor care beyond to-day.

Thomas Gray

Like fruit, children are sweetest just before they turn bad.

Dena Groquet

The beauty of "spacing" children many years apart lies in the fact that parents have time to learn the mistakes that were made with the older ones— which permits them to make exactly the opposite mistakes with the younger ones.

Sydney J. Harris

To be a successful father

there is one absolute rule:

When you have a kid,

don't look at it for the first two years.

Ernest Hemingway

Many a good cow hath an evil calf.

John Heywood

The moment you have children yourself,

you forgive your parents for everything.

Susan Hill

A child enters your home

and makes so much noise for twenty

years that you can hardly stand it:

then departs leaving the house so silent

that you think you will go mad.

John Andrew Holmes

Kids are wonderful,

but I like mine barbecued.

Bob Hope

If nature had arranged

that husbands and wives

should have children alternatively,

there would never be more

than three in a family.

Laurence Housman

If there were no schools to take the children away from home part of the time, the insane asylums would be filled with mothers.

Edgar W. Howe

Children are the most expensive form of entertainment.

Mihaela Iosof

Little children, headache;

big children, heartache.

Italian Proverb

You can learn many things from children.

How much patience you have,

for instance.

Franklin P. Jones

Give a small boy a hammer

and he will find

that everything he encounters

needs pounding.

Abraham Kaplan

Normally, children learn to gauge rather

accurately from the tone of their parent's

voice how seriously to take his threats.

Of course, they sometimes misjudge

and pay the penalty.

Louis Kaplan

Children are a

great comfort in your old age.

And they help you reach it faster, too.

Lionel Kauffman

The real menace in dealing

with a five-year-old

is that in no time at all

you begin to sound like a five-year-old.

Joan Kerr

It kills you to see them grow up.

But I guess it would kill you quicker

if they didn't.

Barbara Kingsolver

A baby is an alimentary canal

with a loud voice at one end

and no responsibility at the other.

Ronald Knox

If you want your children to listen,

try talking softly—to someone else.

Ann Landers

There are few things more satisfying

than seeing your children

have teenagers of their own.

Doug Larson

The secret of dealing successfully with a child is not to be its parent.

Mell Lazarus

A parent who could see his boy as he really is, would shake his head and say: "Willie is no good; I'll sell him."

Stephen B. Leacock

Ask your children

what he wants for dinner

only if he is buying.

Fran Lebowitz

Do not on a rainy day,

ask your child what he feels like doing,

because I assure you that

what he feels like doing,

you won't feel like watching.

Fran Lebowitz

Even when freshly washed

and relieved of all obvious confections,

children tend to be sticky.

Fran Lebowitz

The reason why kids are crazy

is because nobody can face

the responsibility

of bringing them up.

John Lennon

No animal is so inexhaustible as an excited infant.

Amy Leslie

Insanity is hereditary—you get it from your children.

Sam Levenson

Somewhere on this globe,

every ten seconds,

there is a woman giving birth to a child.

She must be found and stopped.

Sam Levenson

The simplest toy, one which even

the youngest child can operate,

is called a grandparent.

Sam Levenson

Many a man wishes he were strong enough to tear a telephone book in half— especially if he has a teenage daughter.

Guy Lombardo

A truly appreciative child will break, lose, spoil, or fondle to death any really successful gift within a matter of minutes.

Russell Lynes

Teenagers are people who act like babies if they're not treated like adults.

MAD Magazine

Kids. They're not easy.

But there has to be some penalty for sex.

Bill Maher

Blessed are they that have children,

for they will never be in darkness.

And, as well as leaving the lights on,

they never shut doors!

Etienne Marchal

It is amazing how quickly

the kids learn the operation of the DVD,

yet are unable to understand

the vacuum cleaner.

Etienne Marchal

Oh, high is the price of parenthood,

and daughters may cost you double.

You dare not forget,

as you thought you could,

that youth is a plague and a trouble.

Phyllis McGinley

A parent who has never apologized

to his children is a monster.

If he's always apologizing,

his children are monsters.

Mignon McLaughlin

Diaper backward spells repaid.

Think about it.

Marshall McLuhan

Children should be like waffles—

you should be able to

throw the first one away.

Mary Alice Messinger

I love children, especially when they cry,

for then someone takes them away.

Nancy Mitford

Children are gleeful barbarians.

Joseph Morgenstern

By the time the youngest children have learned to keep the house tidy, the oldest grandchildren are on hand to tear it to pieces.

Christopher Morley

Never underestimate a child's ability to get into more trouble.

Martin Mull

Every generation revolts against its fathers and makes friends with its grandfathers.

Lewis Mumford

Children aren't happy with nothing to ignore, and that's what parents were created for.

Ogden Nash

Even very young children

need to be informed about dying.

Explain the concept of death

very carefully to your child.

This will make threatening him

much more effective.

P.J. O'Rourke

Humans are the only animals

that have children on purpose

with the exception of guppies,

who like to eat theirs.

P.J. O'Rourke

The quickest way for a parent

to get a child's attention

is to sit down and look comfortable.

Lane Olinhouse

Do your kids a favor—don't have any.

Robert Orben

I take my children everywhere, but they always find their way back home.

Robert Orben

One can love a child, perhaps, more deeply than one can love another adult, but it is rash to assume that the child feels any love in return.

George Orwell

Like all parents, my husband and I

just do the best we can,

and hold our breath, and hope

we've set aside enough money

to pay for our kid's therapy.

Michelle Pfeiffer

What ever happened

to the good ole days,

when children worked in factories?

Emo Phillips

Of all the animals,

the boy is the most unmanageable.

Plato

When you're 12

you no longer need parents.

Roman Polanski

First you have to teach a child to talk,

then you have to teach it to be quiet.

Prochnow

Children and drunks

always speak the truth.

Proverb

Parents, just keep in mind that kids will always round off to the nearest obscenity.

Ray Romano

When you wake up one day and say, "You know what? I don't think I ever need to sleep or have sex again." Congratulations, you're ready (to have children).

Ray Romano

Elephants and grandchildren never forget.

Andy Rooney

I want to have children and I know my time is running out: I want to have them while my parents are still young enough to take care of them.

Rita Rudner

My husband and I are either going to buy a dog or have a child. We can't decide whether to ruin our carpet or ruin our lives.

Rita Rudner

Parents like the idea of kids, they just don't like their kids.

Morley Safer

Children are given to us

to discourage our better emotions.

Saki

There is no such thing

as fun for the whole family.

Jerry Seinfeld

How sharper than a serpent's tooth it is to have a thankless child.

William Shakespeare

Youth is wasted on the young.

George Bernard Shaw

Any kid will run any errand for you if you ask at bedtime.

Red Skelton

What's more enchanting than the voices of young people, when you can't hear what they say?

Logan Pearsall Smith

Bringing up teenagers is like sweeping back ocean waves with a frazzled broom—the inundation of outside influences never stops. Whatever the lure, cars, easy money, cigarettes, drugs, booze, crime, sex—much that glitters along the shore has a thousand times the appeal of a parent's lecture.

Mary Ellen Snodgrass

Children today are tyrants. They contradict their parents, gobble their food, and tyrannize their teachers.

Socrates

There are only two things

a child will share willingly—

communicable diseases

and his mother's age.

Benjamin Spock

Children are a torment and nothing else.

Leo Tolstoy

A baby is an inestimable blessing and bother.

Mark Twain

A soiled child with a neglected nose cannot be consciously regarded as a thing of beauty.

Mark Twain

Familiarity breads contempt—

and children.

Mark Twain

Parents are the bones on which

children cut their teeth.

Peter Ustinov

I don't have any children;

I have four middle-aged people.

Dick Van Dyke

An ugly baby is a very nasty object—

and the prettiest is frightful.

Queen Victoria

Never have children, only grandchildren.

Gore Vidal

By the time a man realizes

that maybe his father was right,

he usually has a son

who thinks he's wrong.

Charles Wadsworth

My unhealthy affection

for my second daughter has waned.

Now I despise

all my seven children equally.

Evelyn Waugh

Children begin by loving their parents.

After a time they judge them.

Rarely, if ever, do they forgive them.

Oscar Wilde

The old believe everything,

the middle-aged suspect everything,

the young know everything.

Oscar Wilde

Winning children

(who appear so guileless)

are children who have discovered

how effective charm and modesty and

a delicately calculated spontaneity

are in winning what they want.

Thornton Wilder

Before I was married,

I had a hundred theories about

raising children and no children.

Now, I have three children

and no theories.

John Wilmot

Small children disturb your sleep,

big children your life.

Yiddish Proverb

What is a home without children?

Quiet.

Henny Youngman

INDEX

A
Adam, James T., 5
Adams, Joey, 5
Aidoo, Ama Ata, 6
Amis, Kingsley, 6
Anonymous, 7-23
African Proverb, 23
Arab Proverb, 24
Armey, Dick, 24
Asner, Ed, 25

B
Baker, Russell, 25
Barry, Dave, 26-27
Baldwin, James, 27
Ball, Lucille, 28
Barr, Roseanne, 28-29
Beecher, Henry Ward, 29
Benchley, Robert, 30
Bensley, Jill, 30
Berger, Ben, 31
Berle, Milton, 31
Bernstein, Al, 32
Billings, Josh, 32
Bombeck, Erma, 33-37
Broyard, Anatole, 37
Bruyère, Jean de La, 38
Burke, Leo J., 38
Burns, George, 39
Bus, Ralph, 39
Butler, Samuel, 40
Buttons, Red, 40
Byrne, Robert, 41

C
Capp, Al, 41

Carlin, George, 42
Casson, Johnnie, 42
Chinese Proverb, 43
Cicero, Marcus Tullius, 43
Colbert, Claudette, 44
Colette, Sidonie G., 44
Cook, Ted, 45
Cosby, Bill, 45-47
Cox, Marcelene, 48
Crane, Monta, 49
Crisp, Quentin, 49

D
Darrow, Clarence, 50
Davies, Robertson, 50
Davis, Bette, 51
Dickens, Charles, 51
Diderot, Dennis, 52
Diehl, Ann, 52-53
Diller, Phyllis, 53-55

E
Éclair, Jenny, 56
Effinger, George Alec, 56
Eikenberry, Jill, 57
Emerson, Ralph W., 57-58
English Proverb, 58
Ephron, Nora, 59

F
Fakes, Dennis, 59

INDEX

Fiebig, John, 60
Fielding, Henry, 60
Fields, W.C., 61
Fife, Shannon, 61-62
Franklin, Benjamin, 62
French, Percy, 63
Freud, Sigmund, 63
Frost, David, 64
Fyfe, David, 64

G
Gallagher, Robert, 65
Goethe, Johann von, 65
Gray, John, 66
Gray, Thomas, 66
Groquet, Dena, 67

H
Harris, Sydney J., 67
Hemingway, Ernest, 68
Heywood, John, 68
Hill, Susan, 69
Holmes, John A., 69
Hope, Bob, 70
Housman, Laurence, 70
Howe, Edgar W., 71

I
Iosof, Mihaela, 71
Italian Proverb, 72

J
Jones, Frankin P., 72

K
Kaplan, Abraham, 73
Kaplan, Louis, 73
Kauffman, Lionel, 74
Kerr, Joan, 74
Kingsolver, Barbara, 75
Knox, Ronald, 75

L
Landers, Ann, 76
Larson, Doug, 76
Lazarus, Mell, 77
Leacock, Stephen B., 77
Lebowitz, Fran, 78-79
Lennon, John, 79
Leslie, Amy, 80
Levenson, Sam, 80-81
Lombardo, Guy, 82
Lynes, Russell, 82

M
MAD Magazine, 83
Maher, Bill, 83
Marchal, Etienne, 84
McGinley, Phyllis, 85
McLaughlin, Mignon, 85
McLuhan, Marshall, 86
Messinger, Mary Alice, 86
Mitford, Nancy, 87
Morgenstern, Joseph, 87
Morley, Christopher, 88
Mull, Martin, 88
Mumford, Lewis, 89

N
Nash, Ogden, 89

O
O'Rourke, P.J., 90
Olinhouse, Lane, 91
Orben, Robert, 91-92
Orwell, George, 92

P
Pfeiffer, Michelle, 93
Phillips, Emo, 93
Plato, 94
Polanski, Roman, 94
Prochnow, 95
Proverb, 95

R
Romano, Ray, 96
Rooney, Andy, 97
Rudner, Rita, 97-98

S
Safer, Morley, 98
Saki, 99
Seinfeld, Jerry, 99
Shakespeare, Wm., 100
Shaw, George B., 100
Skelton, Red, 101
Smith, Logan P., 101
Snodgrass, Mary E., 102
Socrates, 102
Spock, Benjamin, 103

T
Tolstoy, Leo, 103
Twain, Mark, 104-105

U
Ustinov, Peter, 105

V
Van Dyke, Dick, 106
Victoria, Queen, 106
Vidal, Gore, 107

W
Wadsworth, Charles, 107
Waugh, Evelyn, 108
Wilde, Oscar, 108-109
Wilder, Thornton, 109
Wilmot, John, 110

Y
Yiddish Proverb, 110
Youngman, Henry, 111

www.ingramcontent.com/pod-product-compliance
Lightning Source LLC
Chambersburg PA
CBHW032010040426
42448CB00006B/574